ACROPOLIS

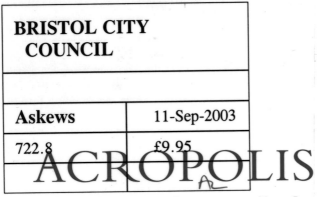

ACROPOLIS

TEXT BY RICHARD ECONOMAKIS • PHOTOGRAPHY BY MARIO BETTELLA

ARTMEDIAPRESS

Richard Economakis lovingly dedicates this book to his wife Elena Ponte

Acknowledgments

Richard Economakis and Mario Bettella would like to thank the Greek Ministry of Culture for permission to photograph the Acropolis Monuments and Museum (1994) and the Committee for the Conservation of the Acropolis Monuments for permission to access and photograph the restoration sites (1994).

They are especially grateful to Professor Manolis Korres for his encouragement in the production of this publication. Many thanks are due to: Dr Charalambos Bouras, Dr Tassos Tanoulas, Dr Cornelia Hadziaslani-Boura, Dr Fani Mallouchou-Tufano, Dr A Papanikolaou, Dr P Calligas, Dr P Zambas, Dr P Kouphopoulos, Dr E Touloupa and Dr Trianti for her assistance with permits. Thanks also go to David Johnson and The Museum of Reconstructions, Inc., for permission to use the computer renderings of the Propylaia. All line drawings have been redrawn especially for this publication by R Economakis and original sources credited accordingly.

Photographic Credits

Unless otherwise stated, all photography by Mario Bettella. The copyright of all photographs granted in 1994 by Mario Bettella to the Publisher of *Acropolis Restoration*, Academy Editions, an imprint of Academy Group Ltd, were reverted to Mario Bettella by Academy Group Ltd's successor in business John Wiley & Son Ltd in 1999.

Front cover: View of the Caryatids on the Erechtheion
Back cover: View of the Acropolis from the northwest, with the Propylaia, Temple of Athena Nike and Parthenon
Page 1: Detail from the east porch of the Erechtheion
Page 2: The Acropolis seen from the southwest
Page 3: Detail of the west pediment of the Parthenon
Page 5: An Athenian 'hoplite', or foot-soldier, being armed for battle (from a 5th century BC vase)

Published in Great Britain in 2003 by ARTMEDIA PRESS
Culvert House
Culvert Road
London SW11 5AP

ISBN: 1 902889 06 1

Printed and bound in Italy

Contents

Introduction

Since its apogee two and a half thousand years ago, the Acropolis of Athens has remained one of the world's most venerated historical sites. The magnificent marble temples and civic buildings that grace the ancient sanctuary, renowned for the beauty of their proportions and their fine details, have been a constant inspiration for architecture and the fine arts. The buildings link us to an age that played a critical role in the formation of Western civilization, one which saw the emergence of Athens as the pre-eminent Greek city state and witnessed the triumph of the Greeks, against all odds, over the invading Persian empire in the early fifth century BC. The Acropolis monuments are living testaments to the leadership Athens in the effort to preserve the freedom of Greece from tyranny and foreign domination. They

Opposite: **The east porch of the Propylaia under restoration with the Caryatids on the right**

also embody the values of the world's first democracy, and the unpre-cedented flowering of the arts, prompted by the new politics of equality.

The universal appeal of the Acropolis monuments is evident in the periodic resurgence of Athenian culture through the course of history, most notably in Roman times, the late Middle Ages, the Renaissance, the Enlightenment, and the nineteenth century. The Romans consciously emulated the architecture of the Acropolis, as did (albeit indirectly) the Republics of Florence, Rome and Venice in the fifteenth and sixteenth centuries. The 'rediscovery' of the Acropolis by Western travellers in the eighteenth century inspired the Neoclassical and Romantic movements in the arts that spread rapidly across Europe and the New World. Today imitations of the Parthenon, Erechtheion, Temple of Athena Nike and Propylaia can be found in just about every major Western city and around the world.

A combination of familiar latinized spellings of Greek words and names and more contemporary phonetic renditions of Greek have been used in this book.

The Parthenon from the northeast

Mythology

The ancient Athenians considered themselves to be autochthonous, or indigenous people, claiming descent from the mythical first kings Cecrops and Cranaos. Cecrops, said to have been born of the earth with a serpent-like lower body, witnessed the famous contest between the deities Athena and Poseidon for patronage of the city. The god Poseidon claimed Athens by thrusting his trident into the middle of the Acropolis and producing a pool of salt water. Athena, instead, planted an olive tree at a spot to the west of the Erechtheion and this was judged by Cecrops to be the better gift.

The half-serpent Athenian ancestor and younger contemporary of Cecrops, Erichthonios, was born from the semen of the god Hephaestos, as it fell to earth during his attempt to violate

Opposite: Late-nineteenth century restitution of the west pediment of the Parthenon showing the contest between Athena and Poseidon (Acropolis Museum)

Athena. She subsequently undertook to raise Erichthonios and when he came of age he replaced Cecrops as king of Athens. Erichthonios was thought to have erected the first cult statue of Athena on the Acropolis and instituted the annual Panathenaic festival. According to Homer, Athena installed Erichthonios' grandson, Erechtheus, in a temple dedicated to herself on the Acropolis, from which he later ruled Athens.

The legend of Theseus, his birth and ascent to the throne of Athens is one of the most important in Athenian mythology. Son of King Aegeus, he was a linear descendant of Erechtheus. On a visit to the city of Troezen, Aegeus took King Pittheus's daughter Aethra to bed and later, from this encounter she bore him a child, Theseus. When he came of age, Theseus made his way to

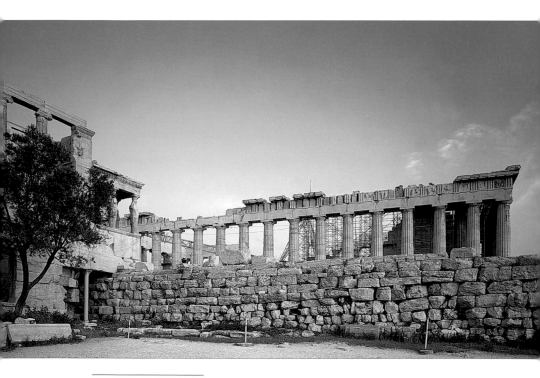

View from the north of the
Parthenon, with the
Erechtheion and replanted olive
tree of Athena on the left

Athens taking with him sandals and a sword which would act as tokens by which Aegeus would recognize him as his son. After successfully defeating a number of dangerous brigands at the Isthmus of Corinth, Theseus attended a banquet given by his father. Fearing him as a contender to the throne, Aegeus attempted to poison Theseus, but on seeing the sandals and sword realized his mistake and dashed the poisoned cup from his son's hands and embraced him as his successor.

Theseus was famous for slaying the half-bull, half-human creature, the Minotaur, that resided in the Cretan Labyrinth. King Minos of Crete had invaded Attica and Athens had agreed to pay tribute to him every year by sending seven youths and seven maidens to be devoured by the Minotaur. Theseus offered to go as one of the sacrificial youths in an attempt to slay the Minotaur. He told his father, Aegeus, that he would change the black sails of his ship to white if he succeeded. In Crete, Minos' daughter Ariadne advised Theseus to tie the end of a thread to the entrance of the Labyrinth so he could retrace his path back from the centre of the maze. Theseus succeeded in killing the Minotaur but forgot to change his ship's sails when returning to Athens. Spying his son's black-sailed ship, Aegeus in despair hurled himself into the sea, which has been known ever since as the Aegean.

Theseus made a number of political reforms. Most importantly, he is said to have created the *synoikismos* of Attica, unifying the tribal settlements and turning them into a single political entity centred on Athens. According to Plutarch, Theseus was responsible for establishing the Panathenaic festival, giving Athens its name, and reinstating the Isthmian Games.

History

Archaeologists have found evidence that Athens has been inhabited from at least the fifth millennium BC. The site would have been attractive to early settlers for a number of reasons: its location in the midst of productive agricultural terrain; its closeness to the coast and the natural safe harbour of Piraeus; the existence of defensible high ground, the Acropolis (from *akron* and *polis*, or 'city on the high ground'); and the proximity of a natural source of water on the north-west side of the Acropolis.

Traces of Mycenaean fortifications from the thirteenth century BC can still be seen on the Acropolis, including some foundations belonging to what must have been a palatial structure. The fortifications, known as the 'Pelasgian' walls (after the indigenous people believed to have built them before the

Opposite: **The western ascent to the Acropolis with the Propylaia and Temple of Athena Nike on the right**

arrival of the Greeks around 2000 BC), remained in use until the Persian Wars of 490–480 BC. One stretch behind the temple of Athena Nike appears to have been deliberately preserved in the Classical period.

There was a decline of Mycenaean society across the Greek world around the end of the twelfth century BC. Whether this was directly connected with the Trojan War (around 1184 BC), or the so-called Dorian Invasion thought to have taken place soon after this conflict, Athens does not appear to have succumbed to an attack. The Mycenaean royal family of Pylos is said to have taken refuge in Athens after their city's fall to the Dorians. One of its members, Codros, became king of his adoptive city.

The collapse of Mycenaean civilization left Greece in political, economic and social decline, accompanied by loss of artistic skills, literacy and trade networks. The Mycenaean form of writing, known as Linear B, was completely forgotten, and the Greek alphabet did not emerge until the late eighth century BC as the new form of writing. At this time city states began

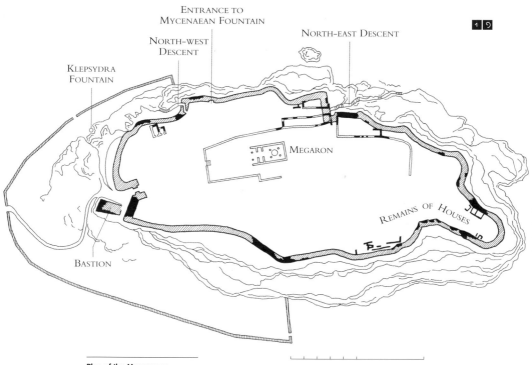

ENTRANCE TO
MYCENAEAN FOUNTAIN

NORTH-WEST
DESCENT

NORTH-EAST DESCENT

KLEPSYDRA
FOUNTAIN

MEGARON

REMAINS OF HOUSES

BASTION

**Plan of the Mycenaean
Acropolis, c. 12th century BC,
after I Gelbrich in J M Hurwit**

to emerge throughout the Greek world, governed by *oligarchies*, or aristo-cratic councils. Thirteen kings ruled in Athens after Codros, until in 753 BC they were replaced by officials with a ten-year term, known as decennial archons, and in 683 BC by annually appointed eponymous archons.

Conflict between the *oligarchs* and the lower classes, many of whom had been reduced to slavery, led to a series of reforms that paved the way for the emergence of the world's first true democracy. Around 620 BC the lawmaker Dracon set up wooden tablets on the Acropolis known as *axones*. These were inscribed with civil laws and punishments so harsh that the death penalty was prescribed even for minor crimes, giving rise to the term 'draconian' which is still used today. Dracon's intervention did little to ensure order, prompting representatives of the nobles and lower classes in 594 BC to appoint the statesman and poet Solon as archon.

Solon terminated aristocratic rule, setting up a representational govern-ment where participation was determined not by lineage or bloodline, but wealth. He eliminated slavery based on debt, and restituted freedom and land to those who had been enslaved. Solon created a 'Council of Four Hundred' from equal numbers of representatives of the Ionian tribes to which the Athenians claimed to belong, and instituted four classes of citizenry.

Peisistratos, Solon's younger cousin, became tyrant (*tyrannos*) of Athens in 545 BC. He ensured the Solonian constitution was respected and governed benevolently. After Peisistratos' death, however, things took a negative turn and anti-Peisistratid sentiment grew. By 510 BC King Cleomenes of Sparta was asked to assist in deposing Peisistratos' son Hippias. Hippias sought refuge in Persia at the court of King Darius.

Soon after, the aristocrat Cleisthenes promised to institute further reforms giving a more direct role to citizens in government. His reforms were passed in 508 BC, and democracy was established in Athens. A new 'Council of Five Hundred' (the *Boule*) replaced the 'Council of Four Hundred', with equal representation from the various tribes. Cleisthenes is

View of the Erechtheion from
the southeast

also credited with instituting the system of ostracism, which 'voted' an individual considered dangerous to democracy into exile for ten years.

It is uncertain when the former Mycenaean citadel was transformed into a sacred precinct but by the late eighth century BC a modest temple (or perhaps more than one) stood on the plateau. The oldest and holiest cult image on the Acropolis was the statue of Athena Polias (Protectress of the City), a crude olive-wood figure, so old that Athenians of the Classical period believed it had either fallen from heaven or been made by Cecrops or Erichthonios. This sacred image of Athena was ritually 'dressed' every year in a *peplos*, a sacred robe, as part of the Panathenaic festival.

A temple is thought to have been built around 700 BC to the south of the later, Classical Erechtheion, to house the statue of Athena Polias. The first major building of which there are significant remains on the Acropolis was the so-called 'Bluebeard Temple', built in the Archaic period around 560 BC. The 'Bluebeard Temple' is thought by some to have stood to the south of the later Erechtheion. Ancient texts mention a mysterious building or precinct contemporary to the 'Bluebeard Temple', called the Hecatompedon, or 'Hundred-footer'. Whatever this structure or place was, it gave its name to the principal room of the Classical Parthenon, perhaps because the later building occupies the same site.

With the expulsion of Hippias a new temple was built on the Acropolis, its foundations still visible to the south of the later Erechtheion. This building, the Archaios Neos, or 'ancient temple', is likely to have been deliberately commissioned around 506 BC as a replacement for the 'Bluebeard Temple'.

The first Persian invasion of 490 BC saw the victory of the Athenians at the battle of Marathon against the forces of King Darius of Persia. The following year the elated Athenians levelled an area on the south side of the Acropolis and began construction of the Old Parthenon. A new gateway to the Acropolis was also commenced, known as the Old Propylaia.

This post-Marathonian building programme on the Acropolis came to a

Top: **Greek 'hoplites', or foot-soldiers, from the Archaic period**
Above: **Archaic limestone 'Three-bodied Daemon' from the
so-called 'Bluebeard' temple (Acropolis Museum)**

violent end in 480 BC when Xerxes, son of King Darius, led a second Persian invasion of Greece. Athens had to be evacuated and Xerxes razed the city and buildings on the Acropolis. Under the command of Themistocles, the Athenians destroyed the Persian fleet in the battle of Salamis. Victory over the Persians was ensured after the battle of Plataea (479 BC), to the northwest of Athens, when a combined Greek army annihilated the Persians.

In the aftermath of the battle of Plataea, a vow was made by the victors never to rebuild the shrines that were destroyed in the war, preserving them instead as memorials for later generations.

Pericles, who was a general

Above: **The Acropolis from the west**
Opposite: **Northern circuit wall of the Acropolis, with
fragments from temples destroyed by the Persians in
480 BC, deliberately displayed as memorials during
the Periclean reconstruction of the sanctuary**

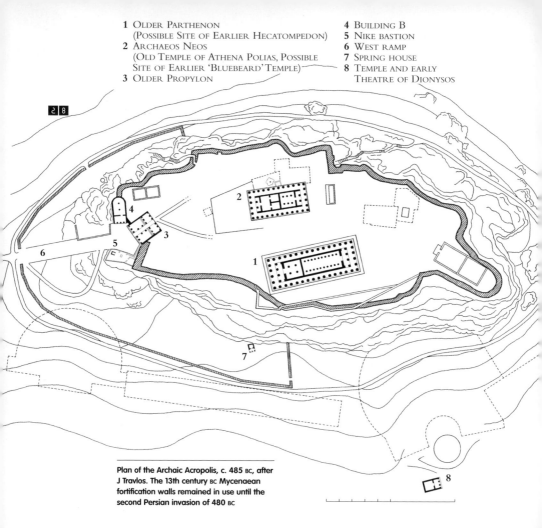

1 OLDER PARTHENON
  (POSSIBLE SITE OF EARLIER HECATOMPEDON)
2 ARCHAEOS NEOS
  (OLD TEMPLE OF ATHENA POLIAS, POSSIBLE
  SITE OF EARLIER 'BLUEBEARD' TEMPLE)
3 OLDER PROPYLON

4 BUILDING B
5 NIKE BASTION
6 WEST RAMP
7 SPRING HOUSE
8 TEMPLE AND EARLY
  THEATRE OF DIONYSOS

Plan of the Archaic Acropolis, c. 485 BC, after
J Travlos. The 13th century BC Mycenaean
fortification walls remained in use until the
second Persian invasion of 480 BC

and statesman, came to power in Athens around 461 BC. He considered the oath of Plataea to have been fulfilled, as thirty years had elapsed from the Persian invasion, and proceeded to reconstruct the temples on the Acropolis. He gathered together the best architects and artists in the city and plans were drawn up to erect new buildings that would outshine those torn down by the Persians. The Periclean building programme enhanced the lower city with new monuments, such as the Temple of Hephaestus, also known as the Theseion, and the Painted Stoa or Poikile situated near the Agora (marketplace).

The Athenian general Pericles

The Classical Acropolis

The earliest major Periclean intervention on the Acropolis was the colossal bronze statue of Athena Promachos by the sculptor Pheidias, whose name would come to be closely associated with the Parthenon. The statue, more correctly known as the Bronze Athena (it is not a 'promachos' type, which would have her striding forward and brandishing her spear), was dedicated some time between 455 and 450 BC. It depicted the goddess helmeted and standing at ease, supporting a shield and spear with one arm, and holding an owl or Nike (winged Victory) in the other. It is also said to have been tall enough (some sources say 30 feet) to catch the light on its helmet and be visible to ships approaching from the direction of Cape Sounion. The Bronze Athena was placed almost exactly on axis and in alignment with the ruined

Opposite: **View of the Acropolis from the northwest, with the Propylaia, Temple of Athena Nike and Parthenon**

Archaeos Neos, as if the goddess herself had stepped forward to remind the Athenians of the tragic fate that had befallen their city thirty years before.

The architects involved in the design and construction of the Periclean buildings went to unprecedented lengths to achieve aesthetic perfection. Their material of choice, Pentelic marble, was a perfect building material: it was relatively easy to carve and could be highly polished. It also created ideal surfaces for painting; we know from surviving examples that Greek temples and sculpture were brightly coloured. The Doric and Ionic mouldings on the Acropolis consisted of simple, unsculpted profiles intended to receive painted decorative motifs. It is likely that after the Persian Wars, the choice of Pentelic marble as the

Opposite: **The Erechtheion and Caryatid porch as seen from inside the Parthenon**

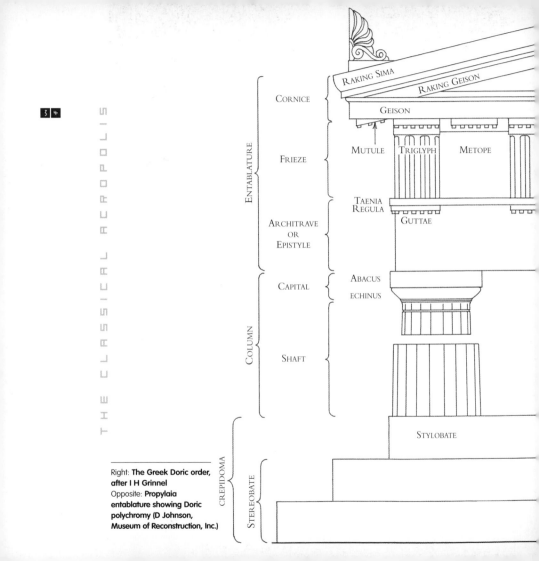

RAKING SIMA

RAKING GEISON

CORNICE

GEISON

MUTULE · TRIGLYPH · METOPE

FRIEZE

TAENIA
REGULA

GUTTAE

ARCHITRAVE
OR
EPISTYLE

ENTABLATURE

ABACUS

CAPITAL

ECHINUS

COLUMN

SHAFT

STYLOBATE

CREPIDOMA

STEREOBATE

Right: **The Greek Doric order,
after I H Grinnel**
Opposite: **Propylaia
entablature showing Doric
polychromy** (D Johnson,
Museum of Reconstruction, Inc.)

principal building material was made by Pheidias and other sculptors in order to achieve a rich polychromatic effect. At the same time the material permitted (in fact, it almost demanded) flawless execution of architectural detail.

The precision of these details on the Parthenon, Erechtheion, Propylaia and Temple of Athena Nike is unparalleled to this day. For example, a typical stone joint on the Parthenon is calculated to be exact to one thousandth of a millimetre. If any joints are visible to the eye today it is due to slight displacements caused by seismic activity, gradual erosion and damage due to acts of war. Of the various refinements worked into the buildings, the most obvious are the horizontal curvature of the Parthenon's stylobate, or stepped platform, which extends right up to the

Opposite: **Typology of temple plans**

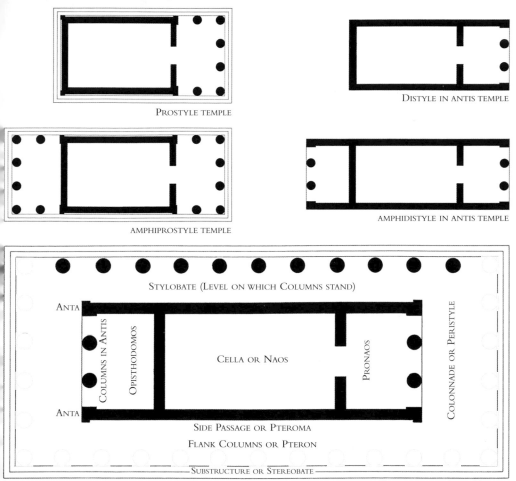

PROSTYLE TEMPLE

DISTYLE IN ANTIS TEMPLE

AMPHIPROSTYLE TEMPLE

AMPHIDISTYLE IN ANTIS TEMPLE

STYLOBATE (LEVEL ON WHICH COLUMNS STAND)

ANTA

COLUMNS IN ANTIS

OPISTHODOMOS

CELLA OR NAOS

PRONAOS

COLONNADE OR PERISTYLE

ANTA

SIDE PASSAGE OR PTEROMA

FLANK COLUMNS OR PTERON

SUBSTRUCTURE OR STEREOBATE

PERIPTERAL IN ANTIS TEMPLE

Above: **Ionic capital from the Propylaia with bronze attachment as conjectured by Manolis Korres (D Johnson, Museum of Reconstruction, Inc.)**
Opposite: **The Greek Ionic order, after I H Grinnel**

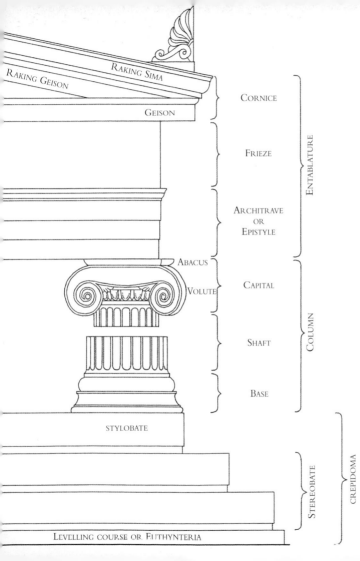

RAKING SIMA

RAKING GEISON

GEISON

CORNICE

FRIEZE

ARCHITRAVE
OR
EPISTYLE

ENTABLATURE

ABACUS

VOLUTE

CAPITAL

SHAFT

BASE

COLUMN

STYLOBATE

STEREOBATE

CREPIDOMA

LEVELLING COURSE OR EUTHYNTERIA

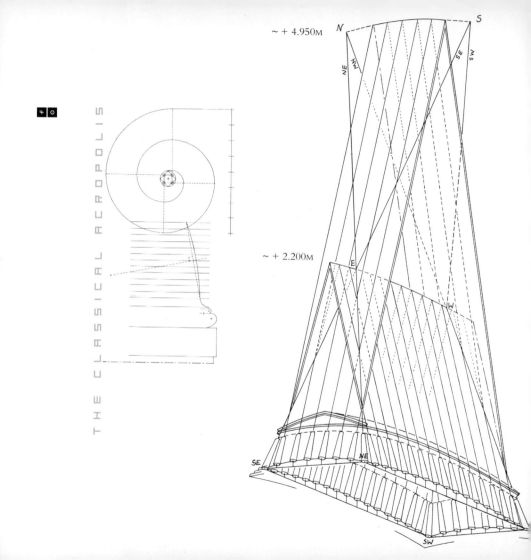

THE CLASSICAL ACROPOLIS

~ + 4.950м

~ + 2.200м

entablature; the inward inclination of the columns, that in the Parthenon meet at precise points thousands of metres above the building; the *entasis* or swelling of the columns and their tapering from bottom to top, creating perfect parabolic profiles; and the subtle thickening of the corner columns to compensate for their apparent diminution when seen against the bright Attic sky. Also, the harmonic ratio of 9 to 4 was used for the critical proportions of the Parthenon. In order to achieve these effects, the architects must have worked them out thoroughly before construction began, every stone surface needing to adjust as the buildings went up. The Parthenon's refinements are thought to have been the subject of a lost treatise on the architecture of the temple which, thanks to the Roman architect Vitruvius, we know to have been written by Ictinos and one Carpion. Such precise and complex planning is a tribute to the remarkable creative spirit of ancient Athens.

Opposite left: **Ancient Greek methods for determining Ionic volutes and column entasis**
Opposite right: **Diagram of the Parthenon after Manolis Korres showing the curvature of the base and inclination of the columns**

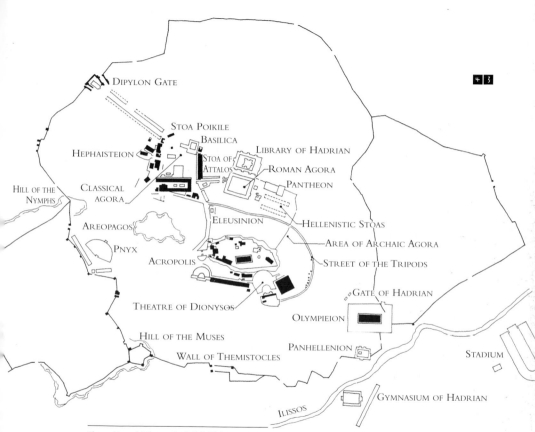

Above: **Map of Athens, after I Gelbrich in J M Hurwit**
Opposite: **The Acropolis as seen from the Pnyx**

1 PROPYLAIA
2 PINACOTHEKE
3 SANCTUARY OF ATHENA NIKE
4 MONUMENT OF EUMENES II (LATER AGRIPPA)
5 NORTH-WEST BUILDING
6 SANCTUARY OF ARTEMIS BRAURONIA
7 CHALCOTHEKE
8 BRONZE ATHENA
9 HOUSE OF THE ARRHEPHOROI
10 ERECHTHEION
11 PANDROSEION
12 FOUNDATIONS OF THE ARCHAEOS NEOS
   (ARCHAIC TEMPLE OF ATHENA POLIAS)
13 ALTAR OF ATHENA
14 PARTHENON
15 ATTALID MONUMENT
16 SANCTUARY OF ZEUS POLIEUS
17 TEMPLE OF ROMA AND AUGUSTUS
18 HEROON OF PANDION
19 ERGASTERION (MARBLE WORKSHOP)
20 KLEPSYDRA FOUNTAIN
21 SHRINE OF APHRODITE AND EROS
22 CAVE OF AGLAUROS
23 ODEION OF PERICLES
24 THEATRE OF DIONYSOS
25 TEMPLE OF DIONYSOS
26 MONUMENT OF THRASYLLOS
27 MONUMENT OF NIKIAS
28 ASKLEPIEION
29 IONIC STOA
30 STOA OF EUMENES II
31 TEMPLES OF ISIS AND THEMIS
32 ODEION OF HERODES ATTICUS
33 SANCTUARY OF APHRODITE PANDEMOS
34 BEULÉ GATE

**Plan of the Classical Acropolis,
modified after I Gelbrich in J M Hurwit**

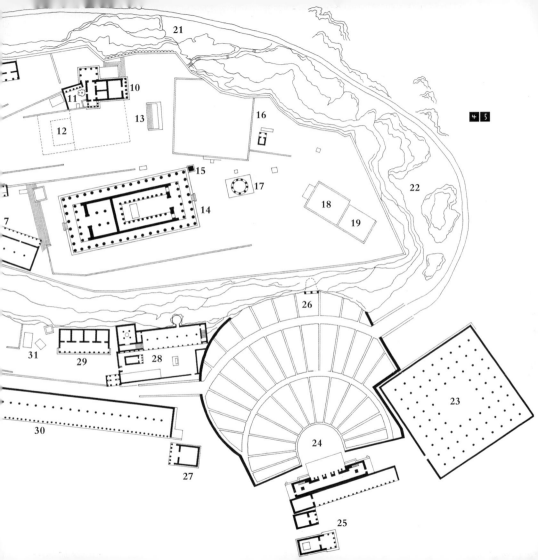

Above: **Aerial view of the Acropolis,
modified after G P Stevens**
Opposite: **View of the Parthenon
from inside the Propylaia**

The Parthenon

Work on the Parthenon, or temple of Athena Parthenos (Virgin Athena), commenced in 447 BC. While Pheidias directed the works with a view principally to the general adornment and incorporation of sculpture, it was the architects Ictinos and (to a lesser extent) Callicrates who were responsible for the construction and architectural refinements of the building. In layout, the Parthenon was a 'double temple' with two unconnected principal interior spaces, similar to the so-called Old Parthenon that preceded it, though it was lengthened by one and widened by two columns. Most of the building rests on the Old Parthenon's massive foundations that had been built on the south side of the Acropolis, with a slight shift to the north and west. Whether or not this influenced the precise proportions of the building, care

Opposite: **The Parthenon from the northwest**

nevertheless appears to have been taken to incorporate into its north colonnade a *naiskos,* or small shrine, and its round altar, which originally stood just beyond the Old Parthenon.

The Parthenon is a peripteral, octastyle Doric temple (ie wrapped by colonnades with eight columns on the short sides) which, like the other Periclean buildings on the Acropolis, is built of fine Pentelic marble. It measures 69.5 x 30.86 metres (228 x 101 feet), and its exterior columns stand 10.43 metres tall. Its length is determined according to the Doric formula of twice the number of columns on the pedimented fronts plus one, ie seventeen. This building displays the characteristic

Above: **West elevation of the Parthenon with photomontage of pedimental sculptures from the Acropolis Museum**
Opposite: **Detail of the west pediment**

1 PERISTYLE (COLONNADE)
2 NAISKOS (SMALL SHRINE) AND ITS ROUND ALTAR
3 ATTALID MONUMENT (2ND CENTURY BC)
4 PRONAOS
5 HEKATOMPEDON (CELLA)
6 STATUE OF ATHENA PARTHENOS
7 PARTHENON
8 OPISTHODOMOS

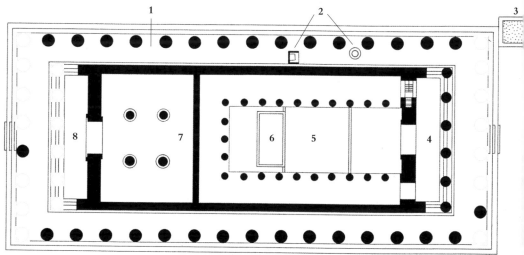

Above: **Plan of the Parthenon after M Korres**
Opposite: **North-west corner of the Parthenon**

THE PARTHENON

View of the north side of the
Parthenon, from the west

features of Doric temples, which are derivative of earlier, timber structures. These include three tall steps at the base, known as the *crepidoma*; fluted, baseless columns with simple capitals, consisting of a square abacus supported by a cushion-like echinus; an entablature, comprising an architrave (representing the principal beam), a frieze with metopes and triglyphs (representing the ends of secondary timber beams) and a cornice, comprising a projecting corona and antefixes. The pediments with their rich sculptures crowned the building's principal short elevations (Greek temples were typically oriented towards the rising sun). The most remarkable aspect of the

Parthenon, South Metope No.27
with battling Lapith and Centaur

The north side of the Parthenon

Parthenon is its sculptures, considered to be among the greatest artistic achievements of the ancient world, and its architectural refinements, including the subtle curvature of the building's base and entablature, and the *entasis* (swelling) of the columns.

As mentioned earlier, the Parthenon is a 'double temple' with two separate principal interior spaces,which are entered through colonnaded porches behind the building's exterior peristyle. The eastern porch, the *Pronaos*, led to the principal cella designed to hold Pheidias' colossal chryselephantine (gold-and-ivory) statue of Athena Parthenos. It is possible to reconstruct this statue on the basis of surviving descriptions and also

Opposite: **Statue of Athena Parthenos inside the Parthenon Cella, modified after C Praschniker**
Right: **Detail of the 'Varvakeion' statuette from the Roman period depicting Pheidias' gold and ivory Athena Parthenos (National Archaeological Museum, Athens)**

© Craig and Marie Mauzy (mauzy@otenet.gr)

miniature copies from the Roman period like the 'Varvakeion' and 'Lenormant' Athenas. It was similar in conception to Pheidias' other colossal figure on the Acropolis, the Bronze Athena. In the Parthenon the triple-crested, helmeted goddess stood in repose, extending a winged victory, or Nike, with her right hand and holding her shield with her left. She wore her famous serpent-fringed *aigis* with its *gorgoneion* (Medusa's head) affixed in the centre. An enormous snake, thought to represent Erichthonios in his role as guardian of the Acropolis, coils menacingly inside her shield. The statue was illuminated by two clerestory windows flanking the

Right: **Detail with pedimental sculptures**
Opposite: **North-east corner of the Parthenon**

Above left: **Interior view of the north-east corner of the Parthenon Pronaos**
Above right: **Exterior view of the same corner**

main cella door and a pool of water or oil in front of it reflected shimmering light back on to the statue.

Another unusual feature of the Parthenon's cella was the wrapping interior colonnade of superimposed columns. Flanking interior colonnades were not unusual in Doric temples but the returning colonnade at the far end of the cella, creating a continuous ambulatory, was an innovation intended to provide an appropriately rich architectural backdrop for the statue while permitting visitors to view it from all angles. The upper colonnade appears to have been accessed by a narrow stair tucked into the thickness of the cella's east wall. Either because it was almost 100 feet in length, or because it occupied the same site as a precinct or temple by the same name, the cella seems to have been referred to in antiquity as the Hecatompedon (Hundred-footer). The western room of the temple is believed to have been a treasury and was probably called 'Parthenon'. In the centre of the room were four tall Ionic columns forming a kind of atrium, though it is unlikely that this was open to the sky.

The incorporation of Ionic columns on the interior of the Parthenon is consistent with other, clearly Ionic influences on the building. These include the slender proportions of the Doric peristyle columns, its octastyle shorter sides and, most famously, the sculpted frieze wrapping the outside of the cella wall. Both the Propylaia and Parthenon – the

Top: **Handing-over of the 'peplos' of Athena, from the east side of the Parthenon frieze, now in the British Museum, after P Connolly**
Above: **East elevation of the Parthenon**
Opposite: **Fragment of the Parthenon frieze from the eastern cella wall showing assembly of the gods (Acropolis Museum)**

THE PARTHENON

South-east corner of the Parthenon

**Interior view of the south-east corner
of the Parthenon Pronaos**

largest and most conspicuous buildings on the plateau – have a Doric exterior treatment, giving the impression that the Acropolis is a Dorian sacred ground. However, it is important to remember that the Athenians considered themselves to be Ionians, unlike most mainland Greek city states which claimed a Dorian ancestry. It is not surprising therefore that the Athenians chose to use the Ionic style for the Temple of Nike, the first building on the way up to the Acropolis, and the Erechtheion, which was the most sacred structure on the summit. Ionic features were deliberately used both in the Propylaia and the Parthenon, probably as expressions of ethnic pride.

Opposite: **South-east corner of the Parthenon**
Right: **Detail with pedimental sculptures**

Today the Parthenon frieze is the most celebrated feature of the ancient temple, though in antiquity it appears to have been less noticed (for example, the ancient traveller Pausanias in his description of the temple makes no mention of it). Its modern fame is due to the fact that little remains of the building's more spectacular pedimental sculpture. The frieze was removed to London between 1802 and 1811 by Lord Elgin, where it exerted a powerful influence on European art and taste. The subject of the frieze is thought to be the annual Panathenaic procession from the lower city to the Acropolis, culminating in the presentation of a new *peplos*, a sacred robe, to Athena at

Top: **Horsemen from the Parthenon frieze, now in the British Museum, after P Connolly**
Above: **The Parthenon from the southeast**
Opposite: **Metopes and triglyphs from the east elevation of the Parthenon**
Overleaf: **South side of the Parthenon**

the temple of Athena Polias, or Erechtheion. Carved in relief by a team of sculptors under the direct supervision of Pheidias, the frieze depicts progressing ranks of mounted knights (probably youths from aristocratic families) with other celebrants and sacrificial animals. It concludes over the Parthenon's eastern door with the handing-over by a child of the sacred *peplos*, in the presence of a large assembly of the gods.

Other greatly admired sculptures from the Parthenon are the metopes, the best preserved of which are from the south side of the temple, depicting scenes from the battle of the Lapiths and Centaurs. Little survives of the pedimental

Opposite: **South-west corner of the Parthenon**
Right: **Interior of the Parthenon cella**

sculptures but we are able to reconstruct them from ancient descriptions and later sketches by Jacques Carrey, a seventeenth-century French visitor who in 1674 was able to record many of the figures still in position. Thirteen years after Carrey's visit, the Parthenon was severely damaged in a huge explosion caused by cannon bombardment by Venetian troops of a Turkish garrison that had turned part of the Parthenon into a gunpowder maga-zine. The east pediment, over the front of the temple, showed the birth of Athena springing fully armed from the head of Zeus, while the west pediment depicted the contest between Poseidon and Athena for patronage of Athens and Attica.

The Parthenon from the northwest

The Erechtheion

The Erechtheion was begun in 421 BC, eight years after the death of Pericles in a plague that killed thousands of Athenians. While the Peloponnesian War did not conclude until 404 BC, a truce (the Peace of Nikias) permitted work to proceed as planned. The Erechtheion was a complex building intended to house the cults of local divinities and heroes that were intimately associated with the Acropolis. More importantly, it was a home to the ancient *xoanon* or wooden cult statue of Athena Polias.

Though there are no extant ancient references to the building's architect, it is likely to have been Mnesicles, who in 432 BC was forced to suspend work on the Propylaia, begun sixteen years earlier, in 437 BC. His authorship is borne out by the incorporation in both buildings of dark Eleusinian marble,

Opposite: **Erechtheion, the Caryatid porch**

the volumetric plasticity, and the clever adaptation to changing

levels in the site. Though work appears to have been briefly

interrupted at one point, construction of the temple was com-

pleted in 405 BC. The following year Athens was forced to sur-

render to Sparta and accept defeat after almost three decades of

fighting in the Peloponnesian War, and endured the humiliation

of a Spartan garrison encamped on the Acropolis. Nevertheless,

for centuries after, the Erechtheion fulfilled its intended purpose

as the sacred focus and culmination of the Panathenaic festival.

The cults of at least ten deities and heroes were pulled

together in this intricate building, which stood out on the north

side of the Acropolis as a sculptural gem to be appreciated

against the massive, simpler Parthenon. It is unlikely that the

---

Opposite: **Plan of the
Erechtheion, after J Travlos**

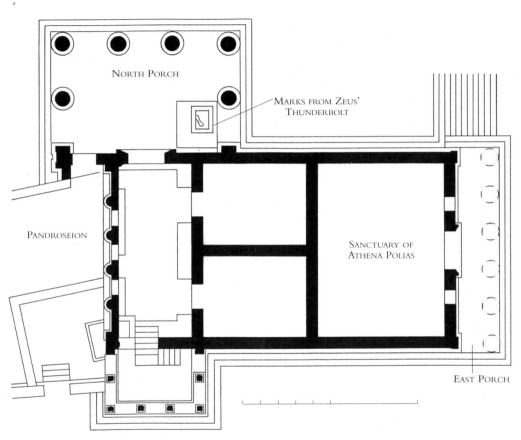

NORTH PORCH

MARKS FROM ZEUS'
THUNDERBOLT

PANDROSEION

SANCTUARY OF
ATHENA POLIAS

EAST PORCH

CARYATID PORCH

Erechtheion was given this name until much later. Originally it would have been known as the Temple of Athena Polias, having replaced a succession of earlier temples to this divinity. It may also have been called Archaeos Neos, in memory of its immediate predecessor on the site, which was torn down by the Persians. Whatever the case, the principal deities to whom it was dedicated were Athena, Poseidon, and (the deified) Erechtheus, first king of Athens, whose tomb was incorporated into the building. The tomb of the legendary Cecrops, and the saltwater spring and trident marks said to have been created by Poseidon in the contest for patronage of Athens,

Opposite: **Caryatids on the west side of the porch**
Right: **The Caryatid porch from the southwest**

Above: **Caryatids with the Hill of
the Muses in the distance**
Opposite: **South-facing Caryatids**

were also contained in the building. The olive tree planted by Poseidon's rival Athena stood in the Pandroseion, a small walled precinct immediately to the west of the Erechtheion. A small enclosure on the bedrock below the pavement of the north porch has curious incisions which are said to be the marks made by the thunderbolt Zeus hurled to separate the quarrelling deities.

Like the earlier Archaeos Neos and the Parthenon, the Erechtheion was a 'double temple' having two inner areas, in this case further subdivided on the west side. Beautifully detailed, this is a highly unusual temple that conforms to no plan types. Its sophisticated juxtaposition of architectural

Opposite: **Caryatids on the east side of the porch**
Right: **The Caryatid porch from the southeast**
Overleaf: **South elevation of the Erechtheion**

elements and volumes make it a masterpiece of asymmetrical design. Of the two pedimented short sides of the Erechtheion, the east was given a prostyle, hexastyle portico (ie porch with six columns). The west cella floor was set some 3 metres (10 feet) below that of the east and approached by a north-facing tetrastyle portico (ie porch with four columns). Little survives of the interior but tentative reconstructions have been made on the basis of ancient descriptions of the building.

From an architectural point of view, the most interesting aspect of the Erechtheion is the way in which the awkwardly located north porch achieves perfect balance when

Opposite: **Erechtheion south elevation from the east**
Right: **South-east corner of the Erechtheion**

THE ERECHTHEION

considered together with the smaller, south-facing Caryatid porch. It is almost certain that this last porch, the Erechtheion's best known feature, was placed on the south-west corner of the building for this purpose, and perhaps deliberately to create an expanse of empty wall to its east. It has been suggested that this blind wall was intended as a place to display the delicately woven *peplos* of Athena at the end of the Panathenaic festival. According to the ancient Roman architect Vitruvius, the Caryatids represented the married women of Caryai, who were enslaved as punishment for their city's decision to side with the invading Persians. In this interpretation,

Right: **North-east corner of the Erechtheion**
Opposite: **East elevation of the Erechtheion**
Overleaf: **The Erechtheion from the northeast**

Opposite: **The north porch of the Erechtheion**
Above: **North porch with bracketed doorway**
Overleaf: **West elevation of the Erechtheion,**
with the replanted olive tree of Athena

the women are condemned forever to support the weight of a stone entablature on their heads, acting as reminders to all visitors of the terrible fate of traitors. However, it is more likely that the Caryatids simply represent *Korai*, or maidens participating in some ceremonial capacity. The little *phialai*, or ointment flasks, that each one holds would seem to support this view as does their relaxed, meditative appearance.

In the early Christian period, the Erechtheion became the Church of Mary, Mother of God. During Turkish occupation of Athens (fifteenth–nineteenth centuries), the building served as a harem for the city's Turkish governor.

Above: **The Erechtheion from
the southwest**
Opposite: **Interior of the
Erechtheion, looking west**

The Propylaia

In 437 BC, a new gateway to the Acropolis, the Propylaia, was begun by the architect Mnesicles. This building was conceived as a monumental backdrop to the conclusion of the Panathenaic procession, an architectural transition from the profane world of the lower city to the sacred ground of the gods watching over it. It was approached by a massive stepped ramp 80 metres (262 feet) long which rose 25 metres (82 feet).

Situated at the edge of the plateau, the Propylaia negotiates an abrupt change in elevation. It comprises two temple-like, open porticoes at different levels – the western portico being lower to align with the end of the ascending ramp. The eastern portico, separated by a series of steps, led through five doorways (*pylai* – hence the plural *Pro-pylaia*). The western portico channelled the

Opposite: **The Propylaia from the south, with the Pinacotheke on the far side**

procession through a narrower passage, defined by a double row of Ionic columns. It is thought Mnesicles chose the Ionic order for symbolic reasons (the Athenians being Ionian Greeks), but also because the more slender proportions allowed him to reach the beams supporting the building's taller ceiling without crowding the interior space. Interestingly, the Propylaia's porticoes were reinforced with iron beams in the architraves.

Flanking the Propylaia's western portico are two projecting, colonnaded wings. These appear to be equal in size but are in fact quite different. The left or northern wing housed the Pinacotheke, a picture gallery thought to have served also as an official dining hall. The south wing is an open, shallow screen intended to mirror the Pinacotheke, creating a symmetrical

Opposite: **Plan of the Propylaia, after T Tanoulas**

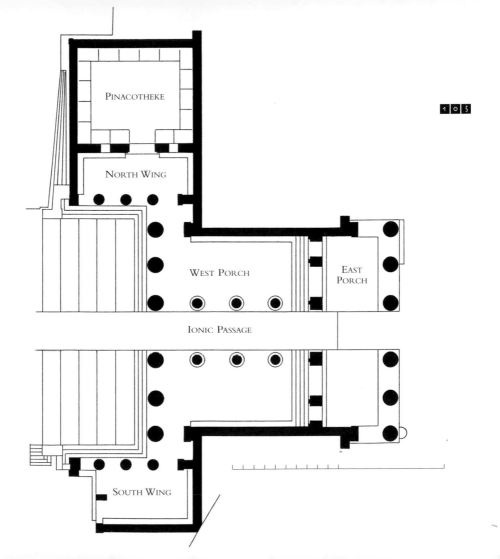

PINACOTHEKE

NORTH WING

WEST PORCH

EAST PORCH

IONIC PASSAGE

SOUTH WING

composition around the entrance portico. Perhaps Mnesicles had intended to extend the building equivalently on this side; if so, he altered his plans so as not to encroach on the site of the little Temple of Athena Nike. He seems also to have deleted from his plans two large spaces intended to flank the eastern portico. Most likely work was suspended due to the outbreak of the Peloponnesian War in 431 BC, which pitted Athens and her allies against Sparta. The Propylaia is clearly an unfinished building. This is particularly evident in the many untreated stone surfaces which even preserve the projecting bosses that were used to hoist the blocks into place.

Right: **The Pinacotheke and monument of Eumenes II**
Opposite: **The west porch of the Propylaia with the Temple of Athena Nike to the right**

Above and opposite: **Panoramic view of the Propylaia from the roof of the Temple of Athena Nike**
Overleaf: **West porch of the Propylaia, with the Pinacotheke on the left**

Above: **The Temple of Athena Nike, seen
from the west porch of the Propylaia**
Opposite: **The south wing of the Propylaia,
as seen from the Pinacotheke**

Views of the Erechtheion (left)
and Parthenon (right) from
inside the Propylaia

View from inside the Propylaia
showing the Erechtheion,
Parthenon and Pheidias'
Bronze Athena, modified after
G P Stevens

Above: **Propylaia, the Ionic passage from the southeast**
Opposite: **East porch of the Propylaia**
Overleaf: **East porch of the Propylaia, from the southeast**
Pages 120 and 121: **South side of the Propylaia, with the Temple of Athena Nike on the left**

The Temple of Athena Nike

The little Ionic Temple of Athena Nike (Victorious Athena) is thought to have been started almost contemporaneously with the Erechtheion around 420 BC, possibly by the architect Callicrates (though some think it was Mnesicles). The smallest of the Periclean buildings, its diminutive size is compensated by its prominent location on the forward bastion, to the left of the ascending ramp leading to the Propylaia. This tetrastyle, amphiprostyle temple (ie two porches with four columns each) was designed to house the Archaic cult statue of Athena Nike, taken away from the Acropolis for safekeeping before the Persians sacked Athens in 480 BC. The Athenians deliberately chose this site for the temple to the victorious patron goddess to convey the message of eventual triumph against their enemies.

Opposite: **The Temple of Athena Nike from the southeast**

Perhaps, too, it is not a coincidence that it aligns with the Pnyx, the great assembly platform to the west of the Acropolis.

The theme of victory was apparent in almost every aspect of the temple's sculptural adornment: bronze winged victories are thought to have stood at the *acroteria*, or pedimental corners; the frieze running around the building shows mythological and historical battle scenes in which the Greeks prevailed; to the west, the pediments depicted the battle between the Greeks and the Amazons, to the east, the battle between the gods and the giants. Enhancing the effect and adding great charm to the building was the Nike parapet that surrounded the bastion. This continuous frieze of beautifully sculpted relief figures of winged victories in various poses, conveyed a relaxed and confident

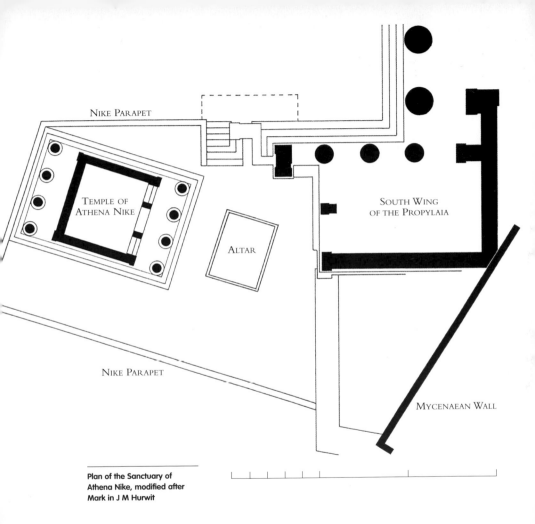

NIKE PARAPET

TEMPLE OF
ATHENA NIKE

ALTAR

SOUTH WING
OF THE PROPYLAIA

NIKE PARAPET

MYCENAEAN WALL

Plan of the Sanctuary of
Athena Nike, modified after
Mark in J M Hurwit

attitude that the Athenians, now only a few years from defeat by Sparta, would not enjoy for long. Two and a half centuries later, in 178 BC, the Temple of Nike was mirrored on the other side of the ascending ramp by the Monument of Eumenes II, King of Pergamon, who had triumphed in the equestrian events at the Greater Panathenaic Games. This 9-metre high, slightly tapering base of grey Hymettian marble originally sup-ported a bronze four-horse chariot. It was rededicated in Roman times to Marcus Agrippa.

Few other Periclean buildings survive on the Acropolis. These included the Great Altar of Athena: a broad, stepped platform a little to the southeast of the Erechtheion (on axis with the older Archaeos Neos) where sacrifices were performed; the Sanctuary

Opposite: **East elevation of the Temple of Nike**
Overleaf: **Temple of Athena Nike from the**
north, with the Hill of the Muses and the
Monument of Philopappos on the right

of Artemis Brauronia to the southeast of the Propylaia, a large open court bounded by a U-shaped colonnaded building where a forest of votive offerings and statues once stood (including a huge bronze rendition of the Trojan Horse complete with life-size heroes peering out from inside it); the Chalcotheke, a colon-naded storehouse for bronze and other metal objects (mostly armour and weaponry), immediately to the west of the Parthenon; the Sanctuary of Zeus Polieus, site of a curious ritual, the *bouphonia* (probably a Mycenaean survival) in which a bull was killed with a double axe, and the axe was then condemned and thrown into the sea; and the House of the Arrephoroi, used by young girls residing on the Acropolis who assisted with the annual weaving of the *peplos* of Athena.

Above: **The Temple of Athena Nike from the south, with the Monument of Eumenes II to the left**

Previous pages: **The Temple of Athena Nike as seen from the western ascent to the Acropolis. The openings in the Nike bastion are thought to preserve a Mycenaean shrine**

Post-Periclean Athens

The Peloponnesian War broke out between Athens and Sparta and their allies in 431 BC, lasting until 404 BC. After Athens' humiliating defeats in 413 BC at the siege of Syracuse (a Greek colony in Sicily, allied to the Spartans) and in 405 BC at the rout of Aigospotami, peace was agreed. The Spartans installed a pro-Spartan oligarchic government called the 'Thirty Tyrants'. These dramatic political and military reversals for Athens at the end of the fifth century BC set the scene for the famous trial of Socrates, who, as his pupil Plato relates, was condemned to death for allegedly corrupting the minds of Athenian youths.

Fourth-century BC Athens once again reached a high level of prosperity, and its artists and intellectuals were renowned across the ancient world. When it succumbed to Philip II of

Opposite left to right: **Horologeion of Andronikos (Tower of the Winds); Odeion of Herodes Atticus; Stoa of Attalus; Monument of Lysicrates**

Macedon at the battle of Chaironeia in 338 BC, the city continued as a great centre of learning. The Hellenistic age that followed the death of Philip's son, Alexander the Great, was one of great patronage of the arts. The ruling Attalids of Pergamon embellished the Acropolis and lower city with numerous fine monuments. Greece fell in 148 BC to the rising power of Rome and many Roman emperors became benefactors of Athens.

Later Classical Acropolis monuments include the Attalid Monument at the north-east corner of the Parthenon (178 BC); the Monument of Eumenes II at the entrance to the Acropolis; and a round, Ionic Temple of Roma and

The Athenian philosopher Socrates

Augustus to the east of the Parthenon. Among the many later Classical monuments built in the lower city are the Choragic monument of Lysicrates (334 BC), the late second century BC Stoa of Attalos II, the Horologeion of Andronikos, or Tower of the Winds (50 BC), and the Arch of Hadrian.

The well-preserved Periclean monuments on the Acropolis owe their condition to continued use in post-antique times. Before the closure of the pagan schools of philosophy by the Byzantine emperor Justinian in AD 529 the Parthenon was transformed into the Church of the Blessed Virgin, and the Erechtheion became the Church of Mary, Mother of God. The Frankish-Florentine period (AD 1204–1456), turned the Acropolis into a home to a succession of Western rulers, most notably the Acciauoli family, who converted the Propylaia into a palace with crenellated tower. When the city was captured by the Turks in the fifteenth century, the Parthenon became a mosque, and the Erechtheion served as a harem. In AD 1686 the Parthenon was used as a gunpowder warehouse for the Turkish garrison,

Bombardment of the Acropolis in 1687 by the Venetian general Morosini, (after Omont 1698)

and it suffered a massive explosion during bombardment of the Acropolis by Venetian general Francesco Morosini. Between 1749 and 1800 the Parthenon was stripped of most of its sculptures by Thomas Bruce, Earl of Elgin, the British ambassador in Constantinople.

Lord Elgin's intention was to record the ancient artworks but he interpreted an ambiguously phrased document from the Turkish occupation authorities as authorization to remove them. Most of the Parthenon frieze, its pedimental sculptures, parts of the Propylaia and Erechtheion, including a Caryatid, are currently residing in the British Museum. Incidents involving Greeks besieging Turks (1821–22), and Turks besieging Greeks (1826–27) inflicted further damage. In the first of these the Greeks offered their enemies ammunition to stop them extracting lead from the clamps in the Parthenon to make bullets. Liberation from Turkish rule in March 1833 saw the Acropolis gradually stripped of its later buildings, restoring it to its Periclean 'Golden Age' glory.

Restoration of the Monuments

A succession of extensive (unfortunately, not always well documented) archaeological excavations were undertaken in the late nineteenth century until 1890, when the Athenian archaeologist Panayiotis Kavvadias with the assistance of German architects Dörpfeld and Kawerau completed the exploration of the entire plateau. By then the Acropolis had been stripped in most places to the bare rock, and its appearance has since remained essentially unchanged. The first systematic restorations of the Acropolis monuments were undertaken in 1898, work concentrating mostly on the Parthenon's western facade.

Until 1933 repairs were effected mostly under the supervision of Nikolaos Balanos, a well-intentioned civil engineer who used countless iron clamps to hold the stones together, without

Opposite left to right: **Cleaning of the columns inside the Propylaia; inclusion of new marble on the south wall of the Erechtheion; titanium clamp replacing an oxidized iron clamp; restoration work inside the Parthenon**

sealing them with lead as the ancient Greeks had done. The iron's gradual corrosion and thermal expansion and contraction caused grievous harm to the Periclean buildings. This damage, together with the effects of earthquakes and the heavy atmospheric pollution of modern Athens, prompted the formation of the Committee for the Conservation of the Acropolis Monuments which, in 1975, began systematic new restorations.

Among the committee's most urgent tasks was the removal of all remaining ancient sculptures and their replacement with cast copies, the cleaning of polluted surfaces, the substitution of Balanos' iron clamps with titanium replacements and the repositioning of newly identified fragments back on the buildings. This last procedure necessitated the occasional inclusion of new marble pieces cut from the same quarries on Mount Penteli that the ancient architects had used. In the process, the Erechtheion and Temple of Athena Nike were entirely dismantled and rebuilt.

Bibliography

Connolly, P. and Dodge, H. *The Ancient City*, London, 2001

Coulton, J.J. *Ancient Greek Architects at Work*, New York, 1977

Dinsmoor, W.B. *The Architecture of Ancient Greece*, London, 1950

Economakis, Richard, ed., *Acropolis Restoration*, London, 1994

Hurwit, J. M. *The Athenian Acropolis*, Cambridge, 2001

Jenkins, I. *The Parthenon Frieze*, Austria, 1994

Kavvadias, P. and Kawerau, G. *Die Ausgrabung der Akropolis vom Jahre 1885 bis zum Jahre 1890*, Athens, 1906

Lawrence, A.W. *Greek Architecture*, revised by R.A. Tomlinson, London, 1996

Orlandos, A.K. *Architektonike tou Parthenonos*, Athens, 1977

Pollitt, J.J. *Art and Experience in Classical Greece*, Cambridge, 1972

Rhodes, R. F. *Architecture and Meaning on the Athenian Acropolis*, Cambridge, 1998

Tournikiotis, J. *The Parthenon and its Impact in Modern Times*, Athens, 1994

Travlos, J. *Pictorial Dictionary of Ancient Athens*, New York, 1971

Richard Economakis is Associate Professor of Architecture at the University of Notre Dame, Indiana. He received his graduate and undergraduate degrees at Cornell University, and has worked as Design Associate with Porphyrios Associates, London. In 2003 he received the Kaneb Teaching Award (University of Notre Dame), and was voted 'Educator of the Year' in 2002 by the AIAS-ND. His experience also includes a number of years as editor of architectural titles at Academy Editions, London, during which time he edited the books *Acropolis Restoration* (Special Mention, Runciman Foundation Awards), *Building Classical*, and monographs on the works of architects Leon Krier and Quinlan Terry. In 2001 he authored the book *Nisyros: History and Architecture of an Aegean Island* (Melissa, Athens).

Mario Bettella is a designer and photographer living and working in London. He has been involved with a large number of architectural publications. His photography is a substantial contribution to many successful titles including: *London*, World Cities Series, Academy Editions; *Building Sights*, Academy Editions; *Acropolis Restoration*, Academy Editions (photographed under the auspices of the Committee for the Conservation of the Acropolis Monuments in 1994) and a number of issues of *Architectural Design* Magazine.